For Alice, Hector, and Tom
N. D.

For Lin
G. B.

The author and publisher would like to thank Michael Kusagak from
Rankin Inlet, Canada, for his input during the preparation of this book.

Text copyright © 2005 by Nicola Davies
Illustrations copyright © 2005 by Gary Blythe

First U.S. edition 2005

Library of Congress Cataloging-in-Publication Data

Davies, Nicola, date.
Ice bear / Nicola Davies; illustrated by Gary Blythe.
p. cm
Includes index.
Summary: Describes how the polar bear, also called Nanuk, thrives in the Arctic
and explains the lessons that the Inuit people have learned from watching the creature.
ISBN 0-7636-2759-3
1. Polar bear—Juvenile fiction. [1. Polar bear—Fiction. 2. Inuit—Fiction.
3. Bears—Fiction.] I.Blythe, Gary, ill. II. Title
PZ10.3.D2865Ice 2001
[E]—dc22 2005046925

2 4 6 8 10 9 7 5 3 1

Printed in China

This book was typeset in Oxalis Alternate DemiBold.
The illustrations were done in oil and pencil.

Candlewick Press
2067 Massachusetts Avenue
Cambridge, Massachusetts 01240

visit us at www.candlewick.com

ICE BEAR

Nicola Davies

illustrated by
Gary Blythe

IN THE STEPS OF THE POLAR BEAR

CANDLEWICK PRESS
CAMBRIDGE, MASSACHUSETTS

Polar bears have longer necks and legs than their closest relatives—brown or grizzly bears.

6

OUR people, the Inuit, call it NANUK.
White bear, ice bear, sea bear, others say.
It's a bear, all right, but not like any other!
It's a POLAR BEAR, made for our frozen world!

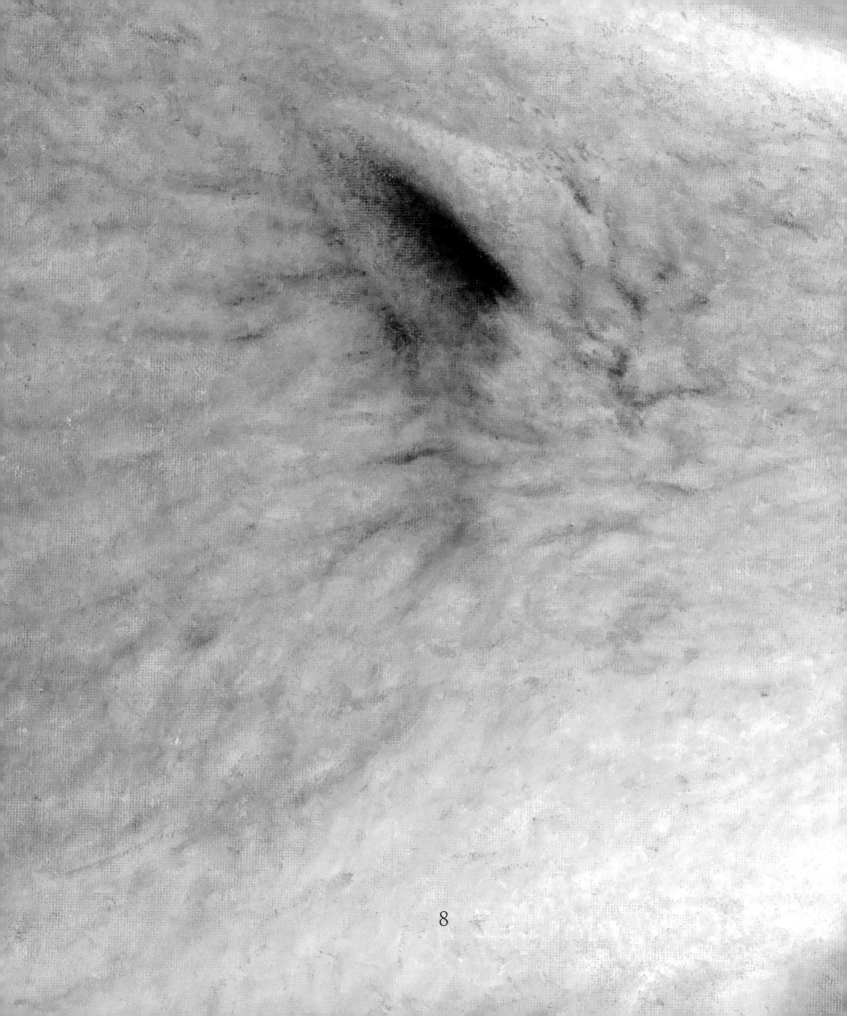

8

No frost can steal **POLAR BEAR**'s
heat. It has a double coat: one of fat,
four fingers deep, and one of fur,
which has an extra trick for
beating cold. Its hairs aren't
really white, but hollow,
filled with air, to stop
the warmth escaping,
and underneath,
the skin is black to
soak up heat.

Only a polar bear's nose and the pads on the ends of its toes are without fur.

Tiny ice crystals rub the dirt from the polar bear's fur.

Polar bears are careful to keep clean so that they stay camouflaged against the snow and ice.

Its ears sit close to its head,
neatly out of cutting winds,
and its feet are furred for warmth
and grip. So POLAR BEAR
stays warm no matter what.
It will sleep away a blizzard in a drift,
and wash in snow.

Polar bears stay warm in temperatures of minus 40°F and lower.

11

POLAR BEAR is a great hunter.
It outweighs two lions
and makes a tiger look too small.

Polar bears are the biggest hunters on land. Male bears can be ten feet long and weigh as much as ten men.

A single paw would fill this page—
and shred the paper with its claws.

It can run as fast as a snowmobile
or walk and walk for days on end.
It can swim a hundred miles without a rest
to cross the sea between the ice floes,
then shake the water from its fur and walk again.

Polar bears' fat keeps them warm in the cold sea.

Webbed feet help them to swim,
and water-shedding fur helps them dry off quickly afterward.

Nothing stops POLAR BEAR.

Polar bears can catch seals only on the sea ice, so hunting is best in winter and early spring.

Seals are its prey.
It hunts them far out on the frozen sea,
waiting at a breathing hole
or stalking them as they sleep.

16

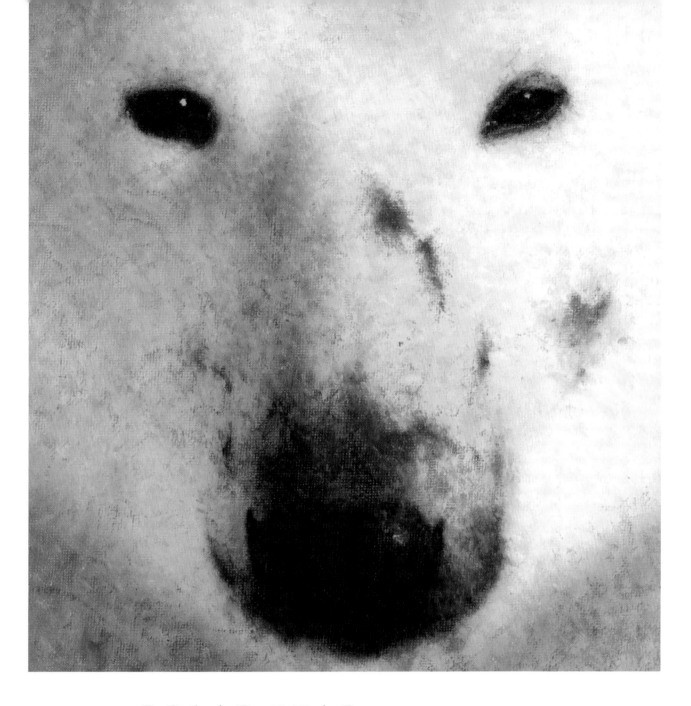

POLAR BEAR is a white shape
in a white world, invisible until it's too late.
A lightning paw strike, a crushing bite,
and the seal is gone.

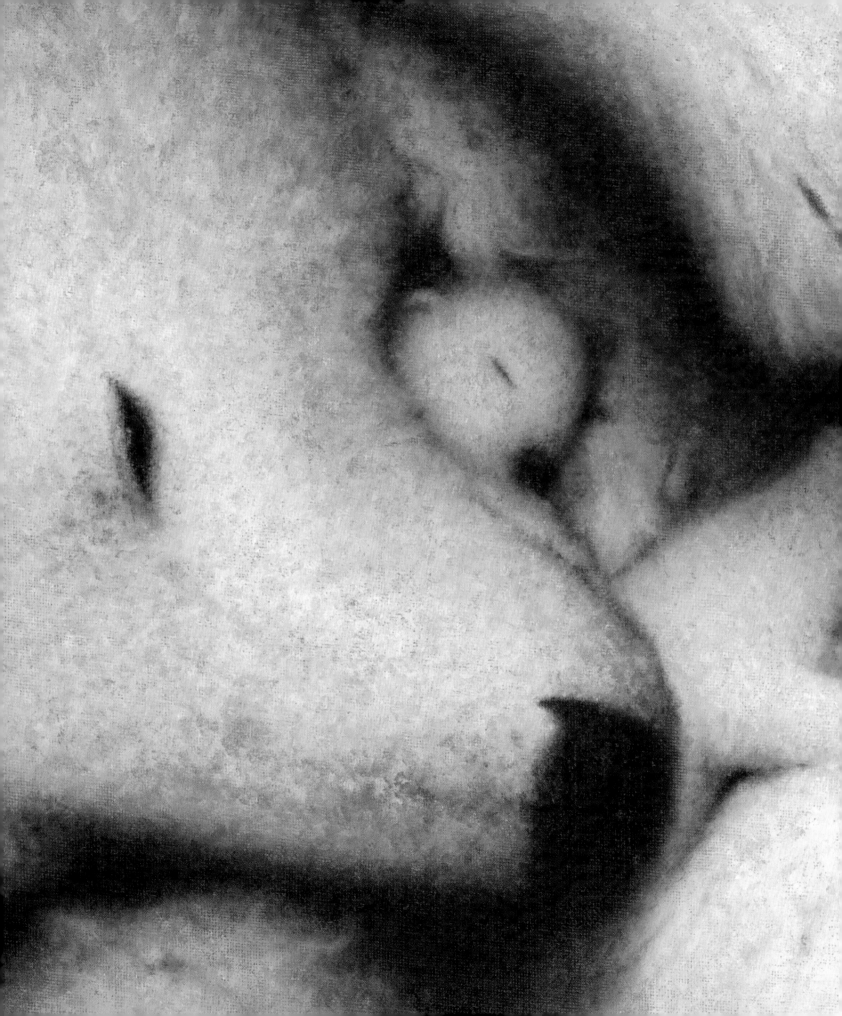

But **POLAR BEAR**
is gentle too.
Mother Polar Bear, in her
winter snow den,
tends her newborn cubs.
She lifts their tiny bodies
in her great paws
and suckles them.

Newborn polar bears are tiny.
They weigh just over one pound—about the same as a guinea pig!

In spring, she'll take them hunting,
and for two years she'll protect and feed them,
until they've learned, like her,
to hunt . . . alone.

Polar bear moms usually have two cubs at a time, but sometimes they have only one or, very rarely, triplets.

21

ALONE . . . through summers, when the sun
tracks up and down the sky and one day
passes to another with no night between.

In the Arctic, it's light all the time in summer
and dark all the time in winter.

When the sea ice melts in summer, polar bears can't catch seals. They'll eat almost anything instead: fish, dead birds, berries, and even grass.

ALONE . . . through winters, when the sun never rises and the stars of the Great Bear sparkle in the darkness.

ALONE . . . until the paths
of two lone hunters cross.
They'll wave their heads in
greeting, clasp jaws so tenderly,
they wouldn't break an egg.
Cautiously, they'll try each
other's strength.
Then? **Play!**
Giants flowing in the
whiteness, tumbling,
beautiful as snowflakes . . .

Real fighting is very dangerous for polar bears!
So males play-fight to find out who's the strongest
without either bear getting hurt.

25

Some scientists think that when humans came to the Arctic around 40,000 years ago, they learned how to survive by watching polar bears.

until they part and slowly go their separate ways.

WE Inuit, we watch NANUK,
as we first watched when the Earth seemed new
and POLAR BEAR showed us
how to love the Arctic—
how to hide from blizzards in a house of snow,
how to hunt for seals with patience and with speed,
how to live in starlit day and sunlit night.

Many polar bears and Inuit have passed since then,
and still we share our world with gratitude and pride.

ABOUT POLAR BEARS

By international agreement, polar bears are protected
wherever they roam. But global warming may be melting
the sea ice they depend on. Here are some things
you can do to help preserve the polar bear's Arctic home:

• Switch off lights, televisions, and computers
when you don't need them.

• Bike or walk instead of getting in the car.

Every little bit helps!

INDEX

camouflage 10, 17

coat 9

cubs 19–21

diet 16, 23

ears 11

fat 9, 15

feet 11, 15

fur 9–11, 15

hunting 12–13, 16–17, 20–23

Inuit 7, 26–27

legs 6

necks 6

nose 9

paws 13

play-fighting .. 25

running 14

size 12–13

skin 9

suckling 19

swimming 14–15

toe pads 9

walking 14

washing 10–11

weight 12–13, 19

Look up the pages to find out about all these polar bear things.

Don't forget to look at both kinds of words –

this kind and this kind.